STAND IN LOVE

TRUTHFUL ANSWERS TO QUESTIONS ABOUT HOMOSEXUALITY, IDENTITY, AND THE CHURCH

Dennis Jernigan

Innovo Publishing LLC
www.innovopublishing.com
1-888-546-2111

Providing Full-Service Publishing Services for
Christian Authors, Artists, and Organizations: Hardbacks, Paperbacks,
eBooks, Audiobooks, Music, and Film

Library of Congress Control Number: 2015953934
ISBN 13: 978-1-61314-307-0

Interior Layout by Innovo Publishing LLC
Cover Design by Israel Jernigan and Innovo Publishing LLC
Discussion Questions & Content Organization by Dani Jernigan

Printed in the United States of America
U.S. Printing History
First Edition: October 2015

TABLE OF CONTENTS

Q: Who Are You to Answer These Questions?

A: Hi. My name is Dennis Jernigan, and I used to identify as homosexual. Through seeking my Maker as to His intent for my identity, I came to the conclusion that I had believed many lies about myself. It has been through my relationship with Christ that I have come to embrace my new identity in Him. I didn't pursue Him to be made heterosexual. I pursued Him to be made whole. Heterosexual thought has come as a result of pursuing wholeness in Christ.

The purpose of this series is to help educate the Church in two things regarding how to respond to today's culture concerning homosexuality: how to respond biblically and how to respond in love. Truth and love go hand in hand, but we must come to the place of understanding God's definitions of love and truth, as opposed to the world's definitions. Historically, the Church has struggled with its response to sexuality. We have tended to lean either toward disgust and hatred or to blanket acceptance and silence. This has left the Church, for the most part, in a state of confusion, bringing ministry in this area to a standstill. Should we separate ourselves from *those people*, or should we offer blanket acceptance, or should we simply adopt a policy of don't ask, don't tell?

I am not a therapist nor am I a counselor. I simply share my story for all those out there who, like me, felt there was something more in this life, and trust me, they are many. I am speaking out for them and speaking to the Church, to the Body of Christ. I heard the call of Jesus, who spoke in this manner to those seeking Him: "If anyone wishes to come after Me, he must deny himself, and take up his cross daily and follow Me" (Luke 9:23). This call applies to those who struggle with unwanted homosexuality, as well as those who don't.

5

Homosexuals are not the enemy of the Church; the enemy, Satan the Liar, is the enemy. As new creations, we have been given vast and mighty weapons of warfare by which to put him down. It is my hope, as you watch this video series and work your way through the study guide, that you will find yourself ready to give an answer when a struggler comes your way, regardless of their particular struggle.

This book is intended as a complement to the video series. Each chapter of the study guide expands on the video content and includes discussion questions to help you and your church work through the many issues surrounding homosexuality and the current culture.

Discussion Questions

1. What are your thoughts and attitudes toward homosexuals right now?
2. Where do you think homosexuals fall in the realm of Christianity?
3. Thus far, what have your attempts to love and share Christ with homosexuals been like?
4. How does your church minister to homosexuals?

Q: Does God Call Homosexual Behavior Sin?

A: Let's make this simple. What does His Word tell us? Leviticus 18:22 says, "You shall not lie with a male as one lies with a female; it is an abomination." You may be saying to yourself, "That's the Old Testament. I thought the New Testament replaced the Law. Does the New Testament call homosexuality sin? Does Jesus call it sin?" In John 10:30, we find the words of Jesus that say, "I and the Father are one." Jesus said that He and His Father were one. That means if God calls homosexual behavior sin, Jesus calls it sin.

God has been setting people free from homosexual sin for a long time. In the apostle Paul's writings to the church at Corinth, he lists a variety of sins. Homosexual behavior is just one among many. Paul says:

> Or do you not know that the unrighteous will not inherit the kingdom of God? Do not be deceived; neither fornicators, nor idolaters, nor adulterers, nor effeminate, nor homosexuals, nor thieves, nor the covetous, nor drunkards, nor revilers, nor swindlers, will inherit the kingdom of God. Such were some of you; but you were washed, but you were sanctified, but you were justified in the name of the Lord Jesus Christ and in the Spirit of our God. (1 Corinthians 6:9–11)

As you can see from this list, homosexual behavior is no different than any other sin. In other words, sin is sin, and Jesus dealt with it all on the cross! Jesus came to seek and save that which is lost. He came for people regardless of their sin. He paid the debt for each and every sinner. My life is one of those that has been changed.

Although it takes one sin to separate us from God, the Word of God does highlight the severity of sexual sin. First Corinthians 6:18–20 tells us to "Flee immorality. Every other sin that a man commits is outside the body, but the immoral man sins against his own body. Or do you not know that your body is a temple of the Holy Spirit who is in you, whom you have from God, and that you are not your own? For you have been bought with a price: therefore glorify God in your body."

The word translated "immoral" in that passage actually means "adultery, fornication, homosexuality, lesbianism, intercourse with animals, sex with relatives," etc. The penalty for such sins was always harsher than ritual uncleanness. The reason for the severity? The human body was intended to be the temple of the Holy Spirit! To defile the temple with sexual immorality was equated with idol worship! How many gods are we to have above the one true God? None!

As the Body of Christ, we are all called to be ministers of reconciliation. Second Corinthians 5:18–19 says, "Now all these things are from God, who reconciled us to Himself through Christ and gave us the ministry of reconciliation, namely, that God was in Christ reconciling the world to Himself, not counting their trespasses against them, and He has committed to us the word of reconciliation." We are called to lead people to Jesus. Jesus is the Savior. Jesus is the Redeemer. Jesus is responsible for the outcome of that life led to Him. We cannot make someone change, but we can lead them to Jesus and, by actively discipling through relationship, help lead them to the Truth of Jesus that ultimately does lead to change. That means that we, as believers, need to be willing to get involved in the messiness of those Jesus calls us to minister reconciliation to. We'll talk more about what that looks like later in this series.

One note, it is very clear what our God's Word calls homosexual behavior; it is sin. Of course, the world would try and alter God's Word in such a way that it appears favorable to sin. The purpose of this video series is to simply take God's Word at face value. If you'd like to learn more about how to refute revisionist or pro-gay theology, read *Pro-Gay Theology* by Joe Dallas.[1]

Overview

1. God calls homosexuality sin in both the Old and New Testament (Leviticus 18:22; John 10:30).
2. Homosexuality is no different from other sins (1 Corinthians 6:9–11). Jesus saved all sinners.
3. God calls us to be ministers of reconciliation (2 Corinthians 5:18–19).
   a. We are called to lead people to Jesus, who can save them.
   b. We are not responsible for the outcome of anyone's life; Jesus is.
   c. We need to be willing to get involved in people's lives.

Further Resources

● Dallas, Joe. "Pro-Gay Theology Overview." Dennis Jernigan (blog), https://www.dennisjernigan.com/needhelp/963-pro-gay-theology-overview.

---

[1] Joe Dallas, "Pro-Gay Theology Overview," Dennis Jernigan (blog), https://www.dennisjernigan.com/needhelp/963-pro-gay-theology-overview.

Discussion Questions

1. Do you find it difficult to call homosexuality sin? Why?
2. To you, does homosexuality seem different from other sin? Do you struggle to accept that Jesus' blood covers homosexual sin just as it covers other sin?
3. What does it look like for you and your church to be ministers of reconciliation to homosexuals?

Q: Do Homosexuals Go to Hell?

A: In Matthew 7:21, Jesus says, "Not everyone who says to Me, 'Lord, Lord,' will enter the kingdom of heaven, but he who does the will of My Father who is in heaven will enter." Romans 3:23 tells us, "For all have sinned and fall short of the glory of God." In Romans 6:23, we find that "the wages of sin is death, but the free gift of God is eternal life in Christ Jesus our Lord." The consequence of willfully continuing in sin is eternal separation from God. It is our choice whether or not we go to hell, whether we practice homosexual behavior or not, whether we practice any sin or not. Jesus is the remedy for sin, pure and simple, whether that sin be homosexual or heterosexual.

When sin has been dealt with, all becomes new. Even after we are saved from our sin, we still face battles of the mind. You see, our battles are not with our bodies, per se, but with our thoughts. Once we come to a place of faith in Jesus, we must actively seek Jesus to renew our minds. It can be done; otherwise, I would not be writing this to you! Sin of any kind is the issue. Willful homosexual behavior is no different than willfully cheating on one's taxes or committing adultery or murder. One sin separates us from God, leaving us in need of a Savior.

The battleground is the human mind. "For as he thinks within himself, so he is" (Proverbs 23:7). Temptation defines no one, yet the enemy of God, Satan, would have us believe that temptation absolutely defines us. The truth is this: a person can be born again yet still battle homosexual thoughts and temptations, but what defines him or her is God. I am who my Father says I am. God looks at the heart and when He sees the blood of Jesus coupled with the repentant heart, He sees one He calls His own. And let's take it a step further; Jesus was tempted in every manner just as we are, yet without sin! Temptation defines no one!

So back to our question, do homosexuals go to hell? All who die without Jesus go to hell, to eternal separation from God. It is not God who sends us to hell ultimately, but we, by our choices condemn ourselves. But we have Good News—great news!—as revealed in John 3:16–18, which says,

For God so loved the world, that He gave His only begotten Son, that whoever believes in Him shall not perish, but have eternal life. For God did not send the Son into the world to judge the world, but that the world might be saved through Him. He who believes in Him is not judged; he who does not believe has been judged already, because he has not believed in the name of the only begotten Son of God.

Overview

1. All sin separates us from God (Matthew 7:21; Romans 3:23). Jesus is the remedy for sin (Romans 6:23).
2. When we are saved, all becomes new, but we still face temptation.
3. The battleground is in the mind (Proverbs 23:7).
4. Temptation defines no one, God does.
5. All who die without Jesus go to hell. We condemn ourselves by our choices.
6. Jesus came not to condemn, but to save (John 3:16–18).

Discussion Questions

1. What sins are most difficult for you to avoid? Which sins seem to define who you are, rather than just what you do?

2. How has your mind been transformed by believing what God says about you? Where do you need to believe what God says, rather than what the enemy says?

3. Can a person be in Christ who struggles with homosexual feelings?

Q: Should Homosexuals Be in Places of Leadership in Our Evangelical Churches?

A: Should a gay person be allowed a place of leadership in a Christ-centered church? Let me put it this way: should a practicing adulterer be allowed to lead the church? Should a known liar be allowed to govern the church? Should a person walking in willful disobedience lead the body? No! First Timothy 3:1–7 says:

> It is a trustworthy statement: if any man aspires to the office of overseer, it is a fine work he desires to do. An overseer, then, must be above reproach, the husband of one wife, temperate, prudent, respectable, hospitable, able to teach, not addicted to wine or pugnacious, but gentle, peaceable, free from the love of money. He must be one who manages his own household well, keeping his children under control with all dignity (but if a man does not know how to manage his own household, how will he take care of the church of God?), and not a new convert, so that he will not become conceited and fall into the condemnation incurred by the devil. And he must have a good reputation with those outside the church, so that he will not fall into reproach and the snare of the devil.

What was expected of the pastor was also expected of those leading underneath him.

Let's go back to that statement regarding leaders being the husband of one wife. In that one clause, many things were implied without being explicitly stated. It was understood that more than one wife was not acceptable. It was assumed that marriage between a man and an animal or between a man and a child were unacceptable. It goes without saying that it was understood that marriage from God's perspective was to be between a man and a woman. Period. It is the wise leader who teaches his flock the mandates of scriptural leadership, and that these mandates be understood by all congregants, whether gay or straight. I would encourage every church to write into their bylaws their stance on, and scriptural reasons for, excluding gay-identified individuals from leadership. I would also recommend writing and documenting policies for marriage being between a man and woman.

Of course, while responding to those who would seek leadership in the church, we must also be prepared for those who fill the pews. Whether we realize it or not, with the recent advent of legalized gay marriage in our nation, we have opened Pandora's Box. What are we going to do when a gay couple with children walks through the door and becomes born again? How do we deal with the aftermath of what that will mean? What are we going to do when a gay congregant passes away, and their spouse wants their gay friends to speak at the funeral or asks a gay friend to sing a gay-affirming song at said funeral? What are we going to do when a gay couple asks to use the fellowship hall for a gay-family gathering? What are we going to do when a gay parishioner sues our pastor for his offensive use of Scripture as hate speech?

And while we're at it, let's address a couple other issues. What about an obedient follower of Christ who is still tempted to homosexuality? Or one who even identifies as gay yet celibate, as someone might identify as an alcoholic, even if they are sober? Temptation defines no one, so we should not identify another by what tempts them. Concerning the one who still identifies as homosexual but chooses to live a celibate life, we must love them and lovingly lead them, through relational discipleship, to find their identity in Christ, until they come to the place of fully embracing who and whose they are.

We must be ready to stand on God's Word, and we must continue to love without compromise, regardless of how confused the world around us becomes. It is in the darkness that the Light is most apparent. Let's just meet people where they are and love them into the Kingdom. That's all we can do, whether we live or whether we die in the process.

In closing, one may be wondering about whether or not gay-identified persons should be afforded church membership. Isn't church membership normally granted to those who profess Christ as their Savior and proclaim new creation as their identity, based upon their denouncement of their old sin-based identity? Church membership is made simple with this admonition from 2 Corinthians 6:14: "Do not be bound together with unbelievers; for what partnership have righteousness and lawlessness, or what fellowship has light with darkness?"

Overview

1. Church leaders should meet biblical requirements (1 Timothy 3:1–7). Verse 2 implies that marriage is between a man and woman. Thus, a practicing homosexual should not hold a place of church leadership.
2. Churches should teach their congregates the biblical mandates for leadership and write policies that clarify their stance on biblical marriage.
3. Churches should prepare to minister to homosexuals by thinking through the many situations that may arise in the coming days.

4. Believers who struggle with homosexual temptation should be lovingly discipled until they fully embrace who they are in Christ.

Discussion Questions

1. Do your church leaders meet the requirements set out in 1 Timothy 3:1–7? Do you?
2. At what point does a Christian who struggles with homosexuality qualify for church leadership?
3. How will your church handle some of the issues laid out in this chapter?
4. How can you help your church wisely minister to homosexuals?

Q: What about Gay Marriage?

A: Those who support gay marriage say things like, "People should be free to love whoever they want." I find it curious that the pedophile community (Yes, there is one.) now uses that same argument. Did you see that one coming? There is a reason that God set boundaries for marriage that entail specifically a man and a woman. Think about it in this manner: do the limits that a computer programmer sets in a program oppress it or free it to operate as intended? Limitations free us to be who we were intended to be. God's divine intent for marriage between one man and one woman is out of His desire of love and protection for us.

Marriage is not merely for the mutual sexual fulfillment of men and women, and it is more than tradition. Marriage must be seen through the filter of the One who instituted it. In Genesis 2:24, we find God establishing marriage with these words: "For this reason a man shall leave his father and his mother, and be joined to his wife; and they shall become one flesh." Marriage was intended for the purpose of perpetuating the human race. It was created by God and should be revered as a holy institution not to be entered into lightly. Husbands and wives are responsible for the vows they make within the covenant of marriage. Mankind has tried to opt out of this God-created institution by doing with it as they desire—according to what *feels* right to them. This abandonment of God-ordained marriage in no way negates the reality of the institution. Like all things not founded and grounded in Truth, the world's view of marriage is bound to fail.

We were created with a need for God. As men and women, we were also created with the physiological need to procreate. Of course, the only way for a man or woman to find real completeness is in relationship with God through faith in Christ Jesus. That being said, within the institution of marriage, God desired to paint a picture of Christ and His Bride. By God's design, marriage was created as a foundational building block of society, with the opposite sexes serving to complement one another. A same-sex marriage cannot do this since both components—male and female—are not present in that marriage. In actuality, same-sex marriage is counterfeit to what God calls holy.

Ultimately, we need completion in Jesus, but God's Word says that it is not good that a man should be alone (Genesis 2:18). Some are called to be single, but many are called to be married. Paul wrote to the church at Corinth that it was better to remain single if the individual had self-control, but also told them that if they had no self-control, they should marry (1 Corinthians 7:1–9). The context was always between a male and female. All people find their fulfillment and completion in relationship with God, but marriage between the masculine and the feminine brings complementation between the sexes. Marriage between masculine and masculine or feminine and feminine prevents complementation. One need but look at the human body to see that male was meant for female and female was meant for male. This is physical completion. If marriage is designed by God, should we not be seeking to discover His design for it?

Jesus spoke directly to God's creation of marriage as being between a man and a woman. In Matthew 19:4-5, Jesus says, "Have you not read that He who created them from the beginning made them male and female, and said, 'For this reason a man shall leave his father and mother and be joined to his wife, and the two shall become one flesh'?" No matter how much the world tries to manipulate what marriage is, it can never duplicate the two becoming one flesh. A man's body is not designed to fit with a man's body, and a woman's body is not intended to fit with that of a woman! Anything outside of God's design is counterfeit!

A man was designed to be fulfilled in marriage by meeting the needs of his wife. A woman was designed to be fulfilled in marriage by meeting the needs of her husband. Each gender has mutual duties toward the other within the bounds of marriage, in spite of what modern thought says.

Wives are instructed to be submissive and obedient to their husbands (Ephesians 5:22–24). What? This is to draw a living picture of the Church submitting to Christ. Submission is an inner attitude; obedience is the outward expression of submission. Submission is an act of humility meant to illustrate the Church-Christ relationship to the world. This does not mean a wife has to do everything her husband says. It would be foolish for her to obey his command to commit sin, for example. This also does not mean that she should be weak, mindless, or unable to make decisions on her own. It simply means that she honors her husband as one who leads her. God-honoring submission is not fearful, foolish, or weak when it is to a husband who is loving and leading as he should.

Now let's think about the role of a man in marriage. Husbands are instructed to love their wives just as Christ loved the Church (Ephesians 5:25–33). This means laying down his life for her. He is to love her as he loves his own body. No man hates his body, but rather, cherishes it and nourishes it. In a very real sense, the husband is a picture of Christ, who loved His bride by laying down His life for her. Love is not a feeling. It is an action. What does love look like? It looks like being a servant. A servant sacrifices his own good for the good of those he loves, giving up comfort, welfare, fulfillment, and earthly goods for the sake of the object of his love—his wife. No room for tyrants or male domination in God's economy of marriage.

Read 1 Corinthians 13 in light of what love looks like, and let your marriage be the epitome of that kind of love. Men, express your love with patience. Be kind. Do not allow jealousy to dictate your expression of love. Don't allow pride to rule your ways. You can love without bragging and without arrogance. Love acts like it values those around it, not acting like a fool. Love is not self-focused or self-centered. Love is not easily provoked to anger. Love keeps forgiving those who offend him. Love does not rejoice in sin. Love rejoices in truth. Love bears all things. Love believes for the best. Love keeps his eyes fixed on hope—on Jesus. Love endures any and every storm life brings. And best of all, love never fails. If men truly valued women as the highly cherished and highly esteemed creations God made them to be, culture would be drawn to this type of covenant, and the world would not need to concoct a counterfeit such as gay marriage.

What makes Christian marriage unique? There are several ways in which marriage, as ordained and created by God, will never change and is different from what the culture says. Godly marriage was intended to be between one man and one woman.[2] Period. In Christian marriage, there is to be no sex outside of marriage.[3] Are Christians perfect in this area? No, but our imperfection does not negate God's design. Sex was designed and intended for the marriage bed.

Christian marriage was created with specific purposes in mind. It was never intended to be based on pure emotion.[4] The world equates love, the feeling, with what God calls love, the laying down of life in covenant. Marriage was created to be the picture of Christ and the Church. This cannot take place in a marriage between two people of the same sex. But God's purposes do not end there. Marriage was also intended to be the framework within which procreation and family were to take place, the framework for nurturing. The world can only counterfeit this area.

---

[2] Brian Hobbs, "Same-Sex Marriage & You: How the Church Can Address Cultural Issues with Grace & Truth" (Keynote presentation at The Gospel, Sexuality, & the Church Conference, Bethel Baptist Church, Anadarko, OK, August 30, 2015), 27.

[3] Ibid., 26.

[4] Ibid., 28.

Marriage was intended to be a lifelong covenant.[5] A covenant in God's economy is simple, saying, I will be faithful to you even if you are unfaithful to Me. Jesus made a covenant in blood—a commitment sealed by His death and resurrection. This truth separates marriage as God intended it from marriage as the world would like it to be. In Christian marriage, we covenant to lay down our lives for each other while the world simply says, "I will love you as long as I feel like it."

Above all, we, the Church, must clean up our heterosexual act as it pertains to marriage. When the divorce rate in the Church is equivalent to that in the world, something is wrong! Christian marriage was intended to convey the relationship between mankind, the Bride, and Jesus Christ, the Groom. Is it any wonder the world scoffs at the institution of marriage when the very beacon of light we were meant to be appears no different than that found in the world? Let us be found faithful, regardless of the world, and regardless of the law of the land. In our Christian marriages, let us be pictures of the Redeemer and His Bride.

Overview

1. Marriage should be defined by God, who created it (Genesis 2:24).
   a. Marriage is intended to perpetuate the human race.
   b. It was created by God and should not be taken lightly.
   c. We are responsible for the vows we make within the covenant of marriage.
   d. Marriage outside of God's parameters is bound to fail.

[5] Ibid., 30.

2. Marriage is a picture of Christ and His Bride.
3. Marriage is the building block of society, with male and female complementing each other.
4. We find completion in Christ, but God said it was not good for man to be alone (Genesis 2:18).
   a. Paul said it was best to remain single, but most people should marry because they cannot control their sexual desires (1 Corinthians 7:1–9).
   b. Completion comes in God, but complementation comes in marriage.
   c. Only male and female can become one flesh (Matthew 19:4–5).
5. Husbands and wives have duties towards each other.
   a. Wives are instructed to be submissive to their husbands in order to display the submission of the Church to Christ (Ephesians 5:22–24).
   b. Husbands are instructed to love their wives in order to display the way Christ laid down His life for the Church (Ephesians 5:25–33). (What love looks like: 1 Corinthians 13.)
6. Christian marriage is unique because:
   a. It is between one man and one woman.
   b. It is the only relationship in which sex should occur.
   c. It has purpose.
   d. It is based on biblical love, not the emotion of love.
   e. It is an example of Christ and the Church.
   f. It is the framework for family.
   g. It is a lifelong covenant.
7. Christian marriage should be an example to the world.

Discussion Questions

1. Who are you allowing to define marriage?
2. Do you struggle with the biblical design for marriage?
3. If you are married, does your marriage represent the relationship between Christ and the Church?
4. Wives, are you offended by the concept of submission? What does godly submission look like?
5. Husbands, do you lay down your life for your wife? How? How can you love more sacrificially?
6. How can your church better support couples in having godly marriages?

Q: Does Orientation Equal Identity?

A: According to dictionary.com, orientation is the "ability to locate oneself in one's environment with reference to time, place, and people; the ascertainment of one's true position, as in a novel situation, with respect to attitudes, judgments, etc." When we are lost in a new place, we are not familiar with the environment, so we do not know where we are in relation to our surroundings. We must then do what? Orient ourselves, or *re*orient ourselves. We think nothing of reorientation in this sense, but when it comes to our identities, it's a whole new ballgame. In my own life, I once felt oriented to homosexuality but felt lost in that identity. So what did I do? I decided that I would reorient myself.

We hear so much these days about a person's sexual orientation, as if that is what defines us. If that were the case in my life, I would be defined as a homosexual, fearful, self-focused, raging lunatic, but none of those things defines me, even if I was oriented toward them.

When I was a boy, I had a temper. At the smallest perceived threat or perceived humiliation, I would fly into a rage of angry outburst, lashing out at whoever happened to be in my path. If I did not get my way, I would turn red and shake with anger. My orientation was toward anger. My mom's explanation, even when I was a boy, was that I came by it naturally! She told me on more than one occasion that anger was in my blood due to my fiery red-headed great-grandparents! In no uncertain terms, she was telling me this was my orientation!

As I grew older, I became intensely fearful of being rejected and made it a practice to go out of my way to ensure that people would like me. I needed to be the best at everything so everyone would like me. I was oriented to perform for the approval and acceptance of others, yet that approval-seeking orientation did not, and does not, define me.

During my entire childhood and well beyond my college years, I was oriented to be self-serving, self-seeking, and self-focused. Everything I did and portrayed myself to be was centered around me, my wants and desires, often at the expense of others. This was my orientation, yet I am not defined as a self-centered person any longer.

Jesus Christ gave me a brand-new identity and, in the process of my relationship with Him, showed me that I am not to be defined by my past failures, by my present circumstances, by whatever may tempt me, nor by the gay community. Only One gets to define me—my Maker. When I determined that God would be the One to define me, He quickly reminded me that my original orientation was toward sin, and my particular sin was the behavior of homosexuality, even if that orientation was not by my choice! You see, we do not get to choose what will tempt us, but in Jesus I have been given the grace to choose what is holy and righteous. Orientation does not define me. Never has. Never will.

Jesus was tempted in every manner just as we are, yet without sinning! "For we do not have a high priest who cannot sympathize with our weaknesses, but One who has been tempted in all things as we are, yet without sin" (Hebrews 4:15). This means that temptation does not define us! This also means that, since we were all born oriented to sin, that orientation does not define us either! That's great news! That means if you are oriented to lying or stealing or slandering or harming others or alcohol or drugs, or you fill in the blank with whatever you're oriented toward, that you have been given a way to reorient!

"No temptation has overtaken you but such as is common to man; and God is faithful, who will not allow you to be tempted beyond what you are able, *but with the temptation will provide the way of escape also, so that you will be able to endure it*" (1 Corinthians 10:13, emphasis added). Did you get that? God will not allow us to be tempted beyond what we are able to bear, but makes a way of escape—always. But that way of escape comes via a relationship with Him.

After the Lord set me free and gave me a brand-new identity, the temptation did not suddenly cease in my life. If anything it intensified, but I began to take God at His Word and began to call out to Him whenever temptation would rear its ugly head—still do. He began to remind me to respond out of my new creation nature and to see life from a new point of view, *His* point of view. "Therefore I urge you, brethren, by the mercies of God, to present your bodies a living and holy sacrifice, acceptable to God, which is your spiritual service of worship. And do not be conformed to this world, but be transformed by the renewing of your mind, so that you may prove what the will of God is, that which is good and acceptable and perfect" (Romans 12:1–2).

I was born oriented to sin, true, but that orientation no longer defines me. Just like Lazarus, I walked out of my old dead life as alive as I could be in Jesus, but I was not as free as I was going to be. Jesus told those around the risen Lazarus to loose the grave-clothes from him (John 11:44). He had been tied up in the bindings of death. I did not want to be merely alive; I wanted to be free from my old orientations and ways of thinking. Through a relationship with Jesus Christ, I was set free—am still in process!

Overview

1. Jesus gives us new identities in him, which are not tied to our past failures, circumstances, temptations, or communities.
2. We are defined by God alone.
3. Jesus was tempted just as we are, yet was without sin (Hebrews 4:15). This means our temptations do

not define us! In Jesus, our orientation to sin doesn't define us either!

4. God always provides a way out of temptation (1 Corinthians 10:13).

5. When we are tempted, we need to respond out of our new nature (Romans 12:1–2).

6. We must loose the grave-clothes from us (John 11:44). We need to be freed from our old ways of thinking.

Discussion Questions

1. What are you oriented toward?

2. Does it comfort you to know that Jesus was tempted just as you are?

3. What grave clothes do you still need to be freed from?

4. Does the idea of orientation being part of our old identities change the way you understand homosexuality or think about homosexuals?

Q: Is Change Possible?

A: With the gender reassignment of Bruce Jenner, I felt compelled to set some things, well, straight (pun intended). The gay identity was one I never wanted, and it dawned on me one day that I should seek my Maker as to His intentions for my identity. I decided to choose what He called right over what my feelings, and the world, called right. I chose Truth over comfort and momentary pleasure and found freedom from my old way of thinking. In the process, I found a heterosexual identity! We live in a world where a man, born a man, is celebrated for saying he's a woman on the inside. One would think a man who did not want a gay identity, and found a way to a heterosexual identity, would be welcomed—tolerated—but I have not found the world too open about anything other than, what feels good is right. Choosing righteousness over license is, in this current culture, not to be tolerated. Enough about that.

People often ask me if I am still tempted with same-sex attraction. When I tell them that I still understand that temptation, but it no longer has power over me, their reaction is often, "Then how can you say you're changed? Nothing's different if you are still tempted." Nothing could be further from the truth.

Honestly, I had no choice in determining what would tempt me, but that in no way negates my ability to choose how I would respond to that temptation! In fact, even Jesus did not get to choose what He was tempted by, and He was tempted in *every* manner just as we are, yet without sin (Hebrews 4:15)! We are either always creatures of choice or never creatures of choice. Our humanity has a conscience, which gives us the power to choose. If we could not choose, every man would be a rapist. Every person would be obese. Every person would walk in constant anger. Every person would be hopelessly self-focused and full of pride. We always have a choice as to how we respond to a given situation. Having a relationship with Christ gives us the power to overcome those temptations and to choose wisely much more easily than in our human strength! If temptation defined us, then we would succumb to the statement that, this is just who I am, so I might as well give in and *be* whatever my deepest feeling suggests I am. Temptation does not equal identity. I did not get to choose what I was tempted by—it was just there—but it was never intended to define me. Even without Jesus, I always had the choice as to how I would respond to any given temptation, be it sexual or otherwise—always. It was only when I allowed the temptation to define me that I began to walk in failure and allow it to control me, control my life.

I recall the look and sound and feel of homosexual temptation. I am reminded of it by the media and culture on a daily basis (Does every TV show or movie have a same-sex story line these days? Pretty much). It's in my face. However, that recollection in no way defines who I am. Temptation is a joy. What do I mean? When temptation comes my way in *any* area that could lead me to sin, I simply ask the Holy Spirit, "What is it, Lord?" My reason is simple. The enemy—The Liar, Satan—desires my downfall. Temptation is intended to lead me to that destruction. I turn to God because the temptation has become my signal that God is up to something. Why else would the enemy be after me if not to quell the work of God in my life?

So much time has now passed since I identified as gay that it is actually difficult for me to believe I was ever that way. Of course, The Liar does not want me to forget, so he continues to try to trip me up in key ways, not usually of a sexual nature either. He attacks me in the areas of my continuing vulnerability: my sense of security, my sense of being needed, or my sense of the need for affirmation. All of these areas are now daily met in knowing Jesus. I am now so secure that I do not fear the attacks on my vulnerability, nor do I fear for my security, nor do I fear that others might not think my life significant. Temptation has been relegated to use for the Kingdom purposes in my life.

When temptation occurs, I do not allow it to determine my direction. Temptation is now like a fly that occasionally tries to land on the meal of God's presence in my life. I shoo the pest away with the Word and continue to enjoy the feast of God's abundant presence. My response to temptation has now become: What is it, Father? Your son, Dennis, waits on You, and while I wait, I will apply Your Word to my existence, bathing my being in You.

People can say I am not changed if I still understand temptation in my life, but for the doubters, here is a brief list of exactly what has changed since coming to faith in Jesus Christ:

- My belief system. I once believed I was born gay until I was born again. I no longer believe I was ever born *that way*.
- My mind. I was transformed by the renewing of my mind.
- My sexual preference. I used to be sexually aroused only by men. My sexual needs are now met only by my wife, and I crave her body, by the way.
- My outlook on life. I once was depressed and self-serving. I now look toward Jesus and lay my life down for the King and the Kingdom.

I. Am. Changed. Period.

This song came as a personal affirmation concerning all God has done to bring about change in my life and identity. You can hear this song at https://soundcloud.com/singoverme/i-am-changed-from-the-film.

"I Am Changed"[6]

Verse
Some call me a fool
For daring to say I've changed
But if that makes me a fool,
I wouldn't trade what I've found for anything
I'm changed
Some call me a dreamer
For daring to walk away
From my old way of thinking
My old identity now passed away
I'm changed

Chorus
Changed from who I thought I was
Changed by pure redeeming love
Changed from death to life
And freed from every chain
Changed from old identity
Freed from lies and freed to be who my Father says I
am
He calls me changed
I am changed!

Verse
Some call me a hater for daring to disagree
Come to my own conclusion of who my Father says I
am called to be
I'm changed
Some call me disillusioned

---

[6] Dennis Jernigan, "I Am Changed," Shepherd's Heart Music, Inc., 2014.

Some call it a mental break
But let there be no confusion
I am fully aware
Fully awake
And I'm changed

Chorus
Changed from who I thought I was
Changed by pure redeeming love
Changed from death to life
And freed from every chain
Changed from old identity
Freed from lies and freed to be who my Father says I am
He calls me changed
I am changed!

Overview

1. We cannot choose what tempts us, but we can choose how we respond to that temptation.
   a. Jesus was tempted in every manner, yet without sin (Hebrews 4:15).
   b. We are always creatures of choice.
   c. Relationship with Christ gives us the power to overcome temptation and choose wisely much more easily.
   d. Temptation does not equal identity.
2. Temptation is a joy.
   a. It pushes us to Christ.
   b. It signals that God is up to something in our lives.
   c. Temptation can be used for Kingdom purposes.

3. Our belief systems, mind, sexual preferences, outlook on life, and more can all change through faith in Jesus Christ.

Discussion Questions

1. What tempts you?
2. Is temptation a joy to you? Does it push you to Christ?
3. How has temptation been used for Kingdom purposes in your life?
4. How have you been changed by knowing Christ?
5. Temptation does not define someone. How does that understanding affect the way you view others regarding their temptations?

Q: How Can I Be Salt and Light Yet Be Seen as Loving?

A: Let me tell you what someone did for me. I had a friend who built a relationship with me. He worked at just loving me right where I was. After a period of time, he felt comfortable and secure enough in our relationship to tell me he knew what my struggle was. He confronted me in love, telling me he knew I was battling homosexual thought and behavior. In that moment, I freaked out, actually running away from the house. After I calmed down, he was still there waiting for me. You know what he told me?

He simply said this, "I don't know how to help you, but I know I know the Answer."

I asked him what he meant.

He said, "Jesus is the Answer."

I told him I'd heard that my whole life, but that Jesus had not done anything for me.

He patiently and simply answered, "I believe Jesus is the Answer. I'm so convinced that here's what I'm willing to do. If you'll let me, I'll walk toward Jesus with you. If you need a shoulder to cry on, I'm your guy. If you need someone to yell at when your mind is reeling in frustration, I can handle it. If you fall down, I won't kick you or say, 'I told you so.' You know what I'll do? I'll help you up every time if you'll let me."

He proved his love to me not with those words, but with his faithful actions, and he still walks with me to this day, since 1981!

Matthew 5:13 says, "You are the salt of the earth; but if the salt has become tasteless, how can it be made salty again? It is no longer good for anything, except to be thrown out and trampled under foot by men." Salt is essential for life. It is a seasoning, a flavoring that brings satisfaction, a taste of the life you have. It causes the world to say, "Hmm, that's good. I want

35

some." Salt can cleanse a wound. Salt can preserve. All these qualities are needed and meant to be expressed by the Body of Christ to a dying, tasteless, rotting world around us. You are needed, whether the world thinks so or not! We are commanded to be salt. More than that, it is who we are in Christ!

In Matthew 5:14–16, Jesus says, "You are the light of the world. A city set on a hill cannot be hidden; nor does anyone light a lamp and put it under a basket, but on the lampstand, and it gives light to all who are in the house. Let your light shine before men in such a way that they may see your good works, and glorify your Father who is in heaven." Light is essential for life; think of the sun. Light dispels darkness and brings life. We are meant to light the way to Christ for a world blinded by death and darkness. We are commanded to be light. More than that, it is who we are in Christ!

People will react to salt and light. They will either move toward it or away from it. No one wants their sin exposed. No one wants their wound dealt with if it means pain. No one wants to be told they are wrong about something. No one wants to have their party crashed. The way we can be salt and light and love people at the same time is simple: do what Jesus would do. Love the person right where they are, but love them enough to not leave them there. If you saw someone headed for traffic and did not warn them, would that be right? People are headed for the traffic of sin's destructive nature. We are commanded to warn them. What greater expression of laying down one's life, than to lead people to the redeeming love of Jesus Christ?

The enemy will hate what you stand for, but remember the words of Jesus in Matthew 5:11–12, "Blessed are you when people insult you and persecute you, and falsely say all kinds of evil against you because of Me. Rejoice and be glad, for your reward in heaven is great; for in the same way they persecuted the prophets who were before you."

Remember, you and I are not responsible for the outcome of another person's life, and we are not responsible for their choices, but we *are* responsible to be salt and light. As new creations, that is who we are. Be who you are, Believer.

Overview

1. We are the salt of the earth (Matthew 5:13).
   a. Salt is essential for life. It brings flavor. It is healing.
   b. As believers, we give the world a taste of Christ.
2. We are the light of the world (Matthew 5:14–16).
   a. Light is essential for life. It dispels darkness. It brings life.
   b. As believers, we help light the way to Christ.
3. People will react to salt and light. Some people will be offended, but we can always do what Jesus would do—love.
4. We will be persecuted, but we will be rewarded (Matthew 5:11–12).
5. We are not responsible for another person's choices, but we are responsible to be salt and light.

Discussion Questions

1. How are Christians salt?
2. How are Christians light?
3. What examples can you think of from your own life of being salt and light?
4. Are you hiding your light and flavor for fear of persecution?
5. Practically, what does it mean for you to lovingly be salt and light?

Q: How Do I Love Without Judgment or Condemnation?

A: Let's say you have a heart condition, a slight blockage in the heart's arterial system. The heart continues to pump, and all appears fine. Over time, however, the slight blockage leads to other issues, creating even more blockage, leading to eventual harm or even death. What if you had discovered your heart's blockage, yet willfully lived with it, leading others to ignore the blockages in their own hearts. Suddenly, your disregard has led others into the false belief that their hearts are fine. In reality, though, this blockage—like sin—leads to eventual destruction. Even more, your destructive choices bring sorrow to those you love. Whether we like it or not, our choices affect others. Whether we like it or not, our choices lead others to make judgments about us.

Someone may say to you, how is my homosexual behavior hurting anyone else? Just because we think our actions or attitudes are not harmful to others, does not mean they aren't. God calls it sin. Therefore, it is harmful to be a proponent of sin, regardless of the kind of sin it is.

Remember when the religious crowd of Jesus' day brought the woman to Him who had been discovered in adultery? They demanded that Jesus answer this question: "Now in the Law Moses commanded us to stone such women; what then do You say?" The words of Jesus were simple, "He who is without sin among you, let him be the first to throw a stone at her" (John 8:5–7). None of us is without sin. None of us has the right to condemn another because of their sin, but that does not mean that we are not called to *judge* the actions of another.

We make judgments each and every day without negating the worth of those we judge. We make judgments about right and wrong all the time. According to my friend, Joe Dallas, "I have to judge what's right or wrong. Jesus Himself underscored this when He asked, ['Why don't you judge for yourselves what is right?'] (Luke 12:57). So I have to make judgments, otherwise how can I live my life, raise my children, discern truth, or know what to expect from others? Every moral assessment requires a judgment" [New International Version substituted for King James Version for clarity].[7]

We should judge the behavior of others. If someone approaches me with a gun drawn—threatening to harm me—I make a judgment of that individual, deeming him harmful to my safety. In that judgment, I make a decision to remove myself from that situation. We should judge the words of others. If we overhear someone say they plan to harm another person or group, are we to sit idly by without judgment? We should judge doctrine. If we hear someone leading people astray with the misinterpretation of God's Word, should we not judge in that situation?

But should we judge the eternal destiny of another without knowing the content of their heart and mind? No. Should we judge the thoughts of another when we cannot possibly read their mind and know their thoughts? No. Should we judge the motives of someone without knowing their heart? No. We have every right to proclaim the Word of God and tell people that it is impossible to have eternal life without Jesus. But we should never say things like, "You can never get into heaven" or "You can't possibly be saved."

What people confuse with judgment is often actually condemnation. When we trash the worth of another human being, harm comes. When our purpose is to cause another to feel inferior as a human being, or when we wish harm on another person, we condemn. Real love, God's love, comes without fear

[7] Joe Dallas, "To Judge or Not to Judge?," Joe Dallas Online (blog), June 17, 2015, http://joedallas.com/blog/index.php/2015/06/17/to-judge-or-not-to-judge/.

of punishment. After all, didn't Jesus take the punishment for sin, for one and all?

Condemnation is communicating to an individual that they are worth less than others, by virtue of what we think they think. As Christians, we hate to feel that sort of condemnation because it seems a direct assault on our identities. Would we want others to feel the same way?

For the person who believes he was born homosexual, our assertion of God's Word seems an affront to their core identity. It is our job, as believers, to relationally demonstrate the truth that our core identity comes from God alone. We must relationally show the world God's design for sexuality by living it out in our own lives.

As always, let us love without worrying about the final outcome. We are not responsible for the outcome of another person's life; Jesus is. Let's let Him be Savior. Let's let Him be Redeemer. Let's just be vessels of His love without the judgment of condemnation. Stand your ground, but stand on the truth, without negating the worth of another. It can be done. And don't waste time on trivial matters like: *What will people think if they see me having coffee with a gay couple?* Or, *What will people think of our church if we openly welcome gay people into our fellowship?* Does it matter what others think of us in such matters, when compared to the reality that people—whether gay or straight—need Jesus if they are to have any hope for eternal life in Christ? If they are going to have any hope of knowing the abundance of life in Jesus? If they are going to experience the joy of knowing God or what true freedom looks and feels like? Knowing Jesus is more than simply being granted eternal life! Let us live our lives like we believe that.

Let's get people to Jesus with kindness, and let Jesus worry about changing their lives.

Overview

1. Sin hurts the sinner, can lead others to sin, and hurts those who love the sinner.
2. If God calls something sin, it is harmful to be a proponent of that sin.
3. None of us has the right to condemn another because we all sin (John 8:5–7).
4. Jesus tells us to judge matters (Luke 12:57).
5. We should judge the behavior, words, and doctrine of others.
6. We should never condemn by causing others to feel inferior or by saying that they can't be saved.
7. God's Word is an affront to the homosexual's core identity. We must relationally demonstrate the truth that identity comes from God alone.
8. We need not worry what others will think of us as we love homosexuals.

Discussion Questions

1. Why does Jesus call us to judge the behavior, words, and doctrine of others?
2. Can you think of a time when you've felt condemned?
3. How have you condemned others? Do you need to repent? Seek forgiveness?
4. Why is God's Word so offensive to homosexuals?
5. How can you love and judge without condemnation?

Q: How Do I Walk Relationally and in Love with Someone Whose Life Practices I Strongly Disagree With?

A: As I said previously, we are not commanded to agree; we are commanded to love. There is no sin in befriending a practicing homosexual. Sin only occurs when you take part in that behavior. Jesus did not hang out with the religious leaders of his day; he befriended those society despised, like tax collectors, the crippled, the blind, and prostitutes—the outcasts. We would be wise to do the same. How is someone going to know the love of Christ unless a life is laid down for them?

What does the laying down of life look like? As varied as the Body of Christ and as varied as the needs around us. We simply need to be willing to walk through the messiness of the lives of others: walking with them toward Jesus, listening, supporting, and helping up when they fall. Heading toward Jesus with a struggler is a form of laying down one's life. Don't separate yourself from the world; engage it. Be *in* it, but not *of* it!

How do we engage without compromising who we are? Romans 12:1 and 2 says it like this, "Therefore I urge you, brethren, by the mercies of God, to present your bodies a living and holy sacrifice, acceptable to God, which is your spiritual service of worship. And do not be conformed to this world, but be transformed by the renewing of your mind, so that you may prove what the will of God is, that which is good and acceptable and perfect." In order to prove to the world what the will of God is, we must know who and Whose we are by the constant renewing of our own minds.

What led me to repentance was not someone telling me I was headed straight for hell; I knew that. What I needed was someone to love me sacrificially, without compromising themselves or their convictions. Kindness led me to repentance.

It is when we relationally walk with someone that they see our responses to life. An age-old adage encourages us to "preach the Gospel at all times and when necessary use words."

Jesus was *the* living sacrifice to the world, to those around Him. We are to be the same. Jesus met me right where I was, but He did not leave me there. He patiently pursued a relationship with me, even when I ran from Him. Let's release in us the love of Jesus by meeting people right where they are, but let's love them enough to not leave them where they are. Let us walk with those who are different than ourselves. We can do it. Jesus did, and we are infused with His spiritual DNA as new creations. And let us be reminded of how we came to repentance in the first place. Think about what Paul tells us in Romans 2:4, "Or do you think lightly of the riches of His kindness and tolerance and patience, not knowing that the kindness of God leads you to repentance?"

Do not see homosexuals as any different than anyone else you would minister to. Homosexuals think their identity is wrapped up in their sexuality. Do not attack their identity as they see it. See your end goal as to lead them to Jesus and not as changing them. Jesus is the Light, and He is Hope. He is the One with the power to change. Just love the person, regardless of how they identify themselves. Just love them right where they are and trust Jesus with the outcome. Jesus loved me right where I was but loved me enough to not leave me there. You and I can do the same; just remember to be kind. We can be kind and loving without compromising who and Whose we are.

Overview

1. We are not commanded to agree, but we are commanded to love.
   a. Jesus loved the outcast, the sinner, and the despised.

    b. We need to be willing to walk toward Jesus with another.

2. We can love without compromise by knowing who and Whose we are (Romans 12:1–2).

3. We are to be living sacrifices to those around us, meeting people where they are but loving them enough to not leave them there.

4. It is kindness that leads to repentance (Romans 2:4).

5. Do not try to change anyone; simply lead them to Jesus and allow Him to change them.

Questions

1. Are you able to disagree with others but still love them?

2. Do you know who and Whose you are, so that you can lovingly engage without feeling uncertain of your own identity?

3. How has kindness led you to repentance?

4. Does it seem difficult to love without trying to change another?

5. What would it look like for you to walk toward Jesus with the homosexuals in your life?

Q: How Do We Respond to Someone Who Says, "I Cannot Change. I've Tried. I Still Feel Homosexual. How Can This Not Be Who I Am"?

A: In Hebrews 4:15, we find this about Jesus, "For we do not have a high priest who cannot sympathize with our weaknesses, but One who has been tempted in all things as we are, yet without sin." Jesus, the Redeemer—Jesus, the Savior—was tempted just as we are, yet without sin! What does that tell us? Temptation does not equal identity. Feelings do not equal identity. Jesus was tempted in every manner—*every manner*—just as we are, yet without sinning! This tells me temptation does not define me. Temptation compels me toward Jesus! It has been through seeking Jesus and finding out Who He says He is, that I have discovered who He says I am. In other words, I simply put off the lies of who I thought I was and put on the truth of who Father God says I am.

Healing is a process. Homosexuality wounded me; I sought Jesus. He bound my wounds with the reality of who He called me to be all along as a man. In the process, I changed the way I thought. As my thoughts changed, so did my attitude. As my attitude changed, so did the way I felt. As my thoughts and attitudes and feelings changed, so did my behavior! Why? Because I act according to who I think I am! God changed my identity, making me a new creation!

Use your own story of salvation to explain these truths. You are not defined by your past failures. You are not defined by your present temptations or circumstances. You are not defined by the culture or society. You are not defined by the LGBT community. You are defined by one and one alone, your Maker, your God.

Overview

1. Jesus has been tempted in *all things* as we are, yet is without sin (Hebrews 4:15). This tells us that temptation and feelings do not equal identity.
2. To discover our identities, we need to put off the lies and put on the truth of who God says we are.
3. Healing is a process.
   a. As our wounds heal, our thoughts change. As our thoughts change, so do our attitudes. As our attitudes change, so does the way we feel. As our feelings change, so do our behaviors.
   b. We act according to who we think we are.
4. We can use our stories to explain this truth.
   a. We are not defined by our failures, temptations, or circumstances.
   b. We are defined by our Maker.

Discussion Questions

1. What temptations have you experienced that became part of your identity?
2. Have you found healing in this area as you believe the truth of who God says you are?
3. What has the healing process looked like for you?
4. Are you willing to share this story of healing?

Q: How Do We Respond to Someone Who Says, "You Say You Love Me, but You Don't Support My Relationship with My Partner. How Is That Loving Me"?

A: The world calls love, sexual expression with whomever and whatever feels right at the moment. God's definition is something different! The greatest expression of love is not the sexual expression. The greatest expression of love is the laying down of life (John 15:13). As a follower of Christ, I daily lay down my life—desires and all—to follow Him. If sin leads to destruction, but following Christ leads to life, what seems the best option to you?

God calls your homosexual relationship sinful behavior. I call your homosexual relationship what He calls it, but that does not mean I do not love you. And by the way, I would have this same conversation with someone who was committing adultery, or willfully breaking the law, or having sex with someone before marriage.

Let's turn your question around a bit: if you love me, you will not ask me to violate my conscience. In other words, I am not casting any stones your way. I simply disagree with you. Love does not require agreement. Love requires that I lay down my life to serve you and love you like Jesus, yet without sinning in the process. For me to bless your union would, in essence, cause me to sin. Is that what you want for me? Blessing sin would be sinful for me. Blessing a gay partnership or marriage would be sinful for me, but:

> Are you hurt? I'll help bind your wound with the healing love of Jesus.
> Are you mourning loss? I will comfort you with the hope of Jesus.

47

Are you in need of food or clothing? I'll share what I have, in the name of Jesus.
Are you in need of someone to talk to? I'll listen and respond with the love of Jesus.
Are you feeling alone or abandoned? I will be there with the love of Jesus.
Are you in need of hope? I'll tell you what Jesus has done for me.

Let me ask you this, Church, are you confused and troubled by what God might want for you or from you? Whether we like it or not, we are not here for our own pleasure or own glory. We are here for God's good pleasure and glory, and we are all given the same ministry—the ministry of reconciliation. God's Word says this in 2 Corinthians 5:17–19:

Therefore if anyone is in Christ, he is a new creature; the old things passed away; behold, new things have come. Now all these things are from God, who reconciled us to Himself through Christ and gave us the ministry of reconciliation, namely, that God was in Christ reconciling the world to Himself, not counting their trespasses against them, and He has committed to us the word of reconciliation.

If you are a new creation, we are called to lead others to reconciliation with God. That means we need to be intentional, and we need to be relational. You may say to yourself, "But I do not know the first thing about leading someone out of homosexuality." I have good news for you; that is not your job. Your job is to lead others to reconciliation—to relationship—with Christ. We are no one's redeemer, nor are we anyone's savior. Let us be relational with others, using the unique gifts

God has given us to simply walk with others toward Jesus. And let's let Jesus be their Savior and Redeemer. Let's let Him worry about the outcome.

Overview

1. The world and God define love differently (John 15:13).
2. We can disagree and still love.
3. If someone loves us, they will not ask us to violate our conscience.
4. It is sinful to affirm sinful behavior, but we can still walk lovingly with those who disagree with us.
5. We have the ministry of reconciliation (2 Corinthians 5:17–19). We need not worry about saving anyone. We simply need to walk with others toward Jesus.

Discussion Questions

1. How do you define love?
2. Are you willing to walk toward Jesus with a homosexual struggler? What would that look like for you?
3. How can you further engage in the ministry of reconciliation?

Q: How Do We Teach Our Children the Truth about Homosexuality in the Current Culture?

A: Do you want your children to learn about sexuality from their peers or do you want them to learn it from you? In order for our children to have a proper view of sexuality, they must see it lived out in us.

When our children were old enough to begin asking questions, they were old enough to have those questions answered. I told them enough at that moment to satisfy their curiosity, knowing the day would come when they would need to know more. When teaching a child the truth about sexuality, or gender differences, or marriage, we need to focus on the truth rather than on the lies we wish to protect them from in the first place.

A government agent, when being taught to recognize counterfeit money, is never shown counterfeit money. He or she is trained in the intricacies of real money—to recognize that which is real—rather than focusing on the counterfeit. Why so much focus on that which is real? So that when the counterfeit comes, it is recognized for what it is—counterfeit. We teach our children the truth so that when the counterfeit comes, they readily recognize it.

When it comes to the God-ordained institution of marriage, we must teach our children that God created marriage and designed it with a purpose. Do you, parent or grandparent, know what the purpose of marriage is? Marriage is to be a picture of Christ and the Church. Christ laid down His life for His bride. Husbands, do you lay down your life for your bride?

When it comes to human sexuality, we must teach our children that God created sex and designed it with a purpose. Just as the human race is driven to find food and water to live, we are driven to procreate as well. God made sex pleasurable so that procreation would take place, but not merely for the sake of pleasure. When it comes to the differences between men and women, we must teach our children that God created males and females to be unique, designed with specific purposes in mind. Man is not greater or more valuable than woman. Men and women are equal but have been designed with different traits and gifts. It is the wise man or woman who teaches their children this truth. Can women do everything men can do? Almost everything. Can men do everything women can do? Almost everything. Just because someone *can* do something does not mean they need to. What does this prove? When one is free to operate within the parameters of their God-given design, true creativity and abundant life have the best opportunity to take place.

Anything that operates outside the design for which it was intended will one day fail. This is what we need to protect our children from in today's culture. Like building a house on proverbial sand is the life built on something other than the foundation of God's Word—faith in Jesus Christ. If you want your children to make wise choices, teach them the truth on which to build their lives. If we do this, the lies will be more easily identified and rejected when they appear.

Overview

1. Children should see biblical sexuality lived out.
2. We should answer questions according to the maturity of our children.
3. Teach the truth, not the counterfeit.
4. Marriage is to be a picture of Christ and the Church.
5. Men and women are equal but different.
6. Sexuality is best when it operates within the parameters laid out by God.

Discussion Questions

1. Do you display appropriate biblical sexuality to your children?
2. Does your marriage display Christ and the Church to your children?
3. Are you willing to engage in conversations with your children about sexuality?

Q: How Do I Minister to My Child Who Has Walked Away from the Lord?

A: We raise our children in the truth, yet they sometimes walk away from that truth when they are adults. Why is that? Whether we like it or not, our children are just like us—they are people of choice. We do our best to teach them to make wise choices, but one day, every parent must face the reality that our children, once they leave the nest, must fly on their own.

My recommendation for the parent who has a prodigal child? Trust your child to Jesus. You focus on being Mom or Dad and allow Jesus to be their Redeemer. Allow Jesus to be their Savior. Allow Jesus to calm their storms. You simply be God's child in the midst of the trials of your child. Allow Him to be the good and loving Father He is, believing in the goodness of *The* Father. Believe Jeremiah 29:11, which says, "'For I know the plans that I have for you,' declares the LORD, 'plans for welfare and not for calamity to give you a future and a hope.'"

As parents, we speak life or death to our children. Let us bestow identity and life upon them via the words we speak and attitudes we express. We do not have to agree with our children to express life. Tell them God loves them no matter what.

In the context of homosexuality, or any habitual sin, love without compromising your own convictions or violating your own conscience. Pray for your child, that God would open their eyes to their true needs, and that they would seek to meet those needs through faith in and relationship with Jesus.

A very powerful prayer can be found in Hosea 2:6. The prophet Hosea had married a woman named Gomer, a harlot. Hosea remained faithful to her despite her infidelity to him. The Lord made a simple statement to Hosea regarding Gomer. He said, "Therefore, behold, I will hedge up her way with thorns, and I will build a wall against her so that she cannot find her paths."

In other words, the Lord said He would raise up a spiritual briar patch to thwart the lies of the enemy, which were intended to tempt Gomer to stray from her marriage vows. In other words, the lies had no place to take root in her mind because the spiritual hedge was a constant nuisance to them! We should ask the Lord to do the same for our children, often.

In his letter to the church at Corinth, Paul the apostle responded to a report of sin in the Body in which a man was having an affair with his father's wife. Paul did not beat around the bush in this matter. He said, "I have decided to deliver such a one to Satan for the destruction of his flesh, so that his spirit may be saved in the day of the Lord Jesus" (1 Corinthians 5:5). What did this mean? From my understanding and perspective, it meant that the man's eternal destiny was more important than his momentary pleasure. It meant that the church was instructed to pray, essentially, that the man would be brought to his knees by the deceit of the enemy, leading him to cry out to God for deliverance. We may not like such a prayer, but it is a necessary prayer at times. As a parent, this would be one of my prayers should one of my children walk in willful defiance of God's will.

As parents of prodigal children, we should have the heart of the father in the Parable of the Prodigal Son (Luke 15:11–32). What was his heart? He loved his son in spite of his selfish, immoral choices. He waited patiently for his son to turn back to Him. The father ran to meet him when, via the storms of life, the child was rendered to a state of humility and brought to his knees. He did not berate the child and say, I told you so! He met his son right where he was and celebrated his return home. He lavished his love on his son. He blessed his son when others felt he did not deserve such treatment. The father *did* love, rather than *spoke* love.

If your child has walked away from his or her faith— whether in a same-sex relationship or not—continue to love them. Don't burn bridges. Don't compromise who you are. Be ready to welcome them home. Admonish when necessary. Speak truth within the context of laying down your life for them. Pray a hedge of thorns around them. Ask the Lord to bring them to their knees however He sees fit. Wait in faith for their return. Rejoice at their return. Shower them with blessings when they return. Thank God when they return, and even if they don't.

> We urge you, brethren, admonish the unruly, encourage the fainthearted, help the weak, be patient with everyone. See that no one repays another with evil for evil, but always seek after that which is good for one another and for all people. Rejoice always; pray without ceasing; in everything give thanks; for this is God's will for you in Christ Jesus. (1 Thessalonians 5:14–18)

Overview

1. Our children are people of choice. They may choose to walk away from the Lord.
2. Trust your child to Jesus (Jeremiah 29:11).
3. Bestow identity and life on your child through your words and attitudes.
4. Love without compromising your convictions or conscience.
5. Pray for your child (Hosea 2:6; 1 Corinthians 5:5).
6. Display love to your child in spite of their sin (Luke 15:11–32; 1 Thessalonians 5:14–18).

Discussion Questions

1. Have you trusted your child to Jesus?
2. Are your attitudes toward your child loving, hopeful, and life giving?
3. How can you speak identity and life to your child?
4. What can you do to display your love to your child, despite your differences?

Q: Now What?

A: Now that we've gone through this series of questions, you probably have even more that could have been answered in these pages. Still, we have a foundation of understanding, based upon God's Word, as to how we can approach and respond to the culture in which we find ourselves.

So where do we go from here, Church? Here are some things we must remember, things that I believe are actually coded within our very spiritual DNA, as it were. We are Kingdom citizens first. Let us not forget this truth. We are not here for our glory or pleasure, but we are here for the Lord's good pleasure. Ephesians 2:10 says, "For we are His workmanship, created in Christ Jesus for good works, which God prepared beforehand so that we would walk in them." Let us walk in this truth and allow it to permeate all we say and do regarding the culture. We are ambassadors for Christ and His Kingdom.

Here are some helpful tips of my own, and some I have gleaned from my friend, Brian Hobbs, editor of The Baptist Messenger of Oklahoma.[8] Another great resource with tips about to how to respond to the culture is the book *Onward* by Russell Moore.[9]

Share Your Story

God's Word tells us that the redeemed are to say so (Psalm 107:2). If we who have been redeemed do not tell our redemption stories, how in the world are those in similar bondage

---

[8] Brian Hobbs, "Same-Sex Marriage & You: How the Church Can Address Cultural Issues with Grace & Truth" (Keynote presentation at The Gospel, Sexuality, & the Church Conference, Bethel Baptist Church, Anadarko, OK, August 30, 2015).

[9] Russell Moore, *Onward: Engaging the Culture without Losing the Gospel,* (Nashville: B&H Books 2015).

ever going to know the hope that lies within us? We, as believers, should be prepared to tell our stories. I own my story! No one can take it from me, and I live to give it away so that others might come to know Him! And while we are on this subject, sharing our stories is one of the ways by which we overcome the enemy (Revelation 12:11)!

Present the Gospel simply and from God's point of view. The Gospel of Jesus Christ has been quite sufficient for the past couple of thousand years. Why try to change it? It is quite simple; salvation is a free gift. We are ministers of reconciliation. We need to introduce people to the One Who is love. Tell people about Jesus and do not try to be their Savior or Redeemer, and do not fret over the outcome of their lives. You are not responsible for their choices.

Remember that people do not get to choose what they are tempted by. The enemy uses confusion over identity and temptation to capture the hearts and minds of those he wants to destroy. That is why, in our ministry, and in our warfare, we need to constantly refer people to Jesus by the way we conduct our lives. People tend to watch what we are doing rather than listen to what we are saying. We should share our stories not only through our words but also through our actions.

Spend Time on What Matters

Spend time on what is eternal, rather than wasting time arguing with someone simply for the sake of being right! Listen to what people are saying and go beyond the surface; get to the root of the issue when possible. Ask probing questions like, how did you come to that conclusion? or, what Scripture do you base your conclusion on?[10] When asking questions like this, do so in humility, expressing genuine interest in why and how they came to believe what they believe. In so doing, you will cause them

---

[10] Ibid., 19.

to have to search their own conscience for what they believe. Do not argue with anyone, but realize that there is a difference between debate and argument.

Focus on one area of concern.[11] To tackle every issue at once would be like shouting into a whirlwind. It gets us nowhere. Be like a laser. This idea has helped me when conducting interviews. Someone once gave me sage advice: make the interview your own. Regardless of the question, find a way to get back to the point you are trying to make.

Don't expect too much and do not overreach.[12] Expect a human-centered response from someone who doesn't know Jesus. Keep loving and trusting God to lead them to Truth without you beating them over the head with it!

Concede trivial matters.[13] When I hear people say things like, "The gay community has expressed more kindness to me than the Church ever has," they may be right. Concede such matters and move back to the topic. Some things are worth defending; some are not.

Avoid euphemisms, but don't get bogged down in a language debate.[14] Keep it simple and do not try to overthink the subject matter. Communicate with clarity what you are trying to say. You do not have to water down the Word of God.

Know when to stop.[15] Set boundaries for yourself and do not cross them. Do not allow anger to rule the conversation. Remember this: we can only help people who want help.

---

[11] Ibid., 18.
[12] Ibid., 23.
[13] Ibid., 22.
[14] Ibid., 20.
[15] Ibid., 24.

Be Kind

We have but to go to God's Word to find out how we are to treat people, regardless of whether they agree with us or not.

Treat others the same way you want them to treat you. (Luke 6:31)

Let your speech always be with grace, as though seasoned with salt, so that you will know how you should respond to each person. (Colossians 4:6)

But sanctify Christ as Lord in your hearts, always being ready to make a defense to everyone who asks you to give an account for the hope that is in you, yet with gentleness and reverence. (1 Peter 3:15)

In other words, do not put another person down or belittle them. How would you feel should you be put down or belittled?

When engaging in conversation with someone who is in favor of something opposed to God's will and design, like same-sex marriage, it is important that we bathe everything in kindness. Remember, it was kindness that led us to repentance in our own lives. Kindness is a weapon of our warfare! People are not our enemy; the enemy of God is our enemy.

Expect Persecution

I would be remiss if I did not remind you of one very important component: spiritual warfare. We are at war with The Liar, Satan, and his deception. As Kingdom citizens and aliens in a strange land, do not be surprised when the world rejects Truth. Do not confuse rejection of God and His Truth with personal rejection. You will be rejected, just as Jesus was, but God will use even that rejection to bring others to Himself. Choose to walk in love in spite of how you are treated or perceived by others.

> Beloved, I urge you as aliens and strangers to abstain from fleshly lusts which wage war against the soul. Keep your behavior excellent among the Gentiles, so that in the thing in which they slander you as evildoers, they may because of your good deeds, as they observe them, glorify God in the day of visitation. (1 Peter 2:11–12)

May I remind you that the same God that delivered Shadrach, Meshach, and Abednego from the fiery furnace is the same God that is with us now. May I remind you that the same God that delivered Paul and Silas from prison is the same God that is with us now. May I remind you that Paul affected the entire world from a prison cell in Rome. And may I remind you that whether we live or die, we are the Lord's (Romans 14:8) and that to be absent from our body is to be present with Christ (2 Corinthians 5:8). In other words, we win no matter what!

We live in a litigious culture. We, as Christians, are the ones being threatened. Christian-based businesses are being sought out, and lawsuits are frequently coming against them. What does this mean? We may be sued at some point for our faith. We might as well have a plan for this, or for the day we find ourselves faced with imprisonment due to our unwavering faith in God and His Word. But who is really under attack here? It is not us, but Christ. Let us use the weapons of our warfare as God intended. Pray without ceasing. Let worship permeate your existence and affect all you say, think, and do. Use the name of Jesus, proclaiming Truth into the spiritual realm and atmosphere. And I encourage you to read the end of the Book—we win.

And remember this. Not everything that offends us should. Not everything that we perceive as persecution is really persecution. God will give grace to stand alone when necessary. Do not fret over what tomorrow might bring. God has not changed, and He will not change. He will be with us, whether we live or whether we die. Is your faith something worth dying for? Is Jesus worth dying for? Is the homosexual worth dying for? I think you know The Answer.

God has not changed nor has His grace weakened. Whatever we are called or allowed to go through in this life is not without purpose, and we are never alone. Be of good cheer. God is still, and will always be, on the throne, regardless of what mankind says or does. Trust Him.

Final Thoughts

I wish there were some simple formula to make dealing with the culture as easy as one, two, three. But in one way, there is. That formula is Love—and His name is Jesus. When in doubt about what to do or say, look to Jesus. When you don't know what to say to some hurting soul, point them to Jesus. When you're faced with a difficult cultural situation or circumstance, go through that trial with Jesus. When others call you a hater, love like Jesus, unwilling to compromise the Truth but willing to lay down your life.

Let us meet people right where they are, whether they are in a same-sex relationship or professing to be transgender. Just love them right where they are and have the heart of Jesus. Be willing to walk toward Jesus with those God leads into your life. Be that shoulder to cry on. Be that listening ear that empathizes with their pain. Be that helping hand that picks them up each and every time they fall. Be the salt they need for healing. Be the light they need to see the Truth. Just be who our Father says you are. You are an ambassador for Christ. Let Jesus be their Savior. Let Him be their Redeemer. Let Jesus worry about the outcome of their lives.

When faced with legal action or possible jail time due to your stand on God's Word, expect the grace of God to flood your existence. Expect Him to accompany you with the sweetness of His dear presence, no matter what fiery trials you must endure. The God who delivered Daniel from the lion's den is the same God in your here and now. The Holy Spirit that was with Peter and John and Paul and Silas when they were thrown into jail is the same God that will set us free though we find ourselves bound in chains.

My best recommendation to each believer is simple: we must learn to see each and every aspect of our life from God's point of view. We may see an insurmountable mountain; he sees a molehill that is easily traversed. We may see a raging, violent storm; he sees the opportunity for refuge and peace in the very midst of the onslaught. We may see darkness and vitriol hurled our way; he sees an opportunity to bless those who curse us.

Church, we've been here before. Cultures come and go. Kingdoms rise and fall, but our God never changes! Let us not lose heart, but rather, let us fix our eyes on Jesus and remember why we are even here.

> Therefore, since we have so great a cloud of witnesses surrounding us, let us also lay aside every encumbrance and the sin which so easily entangles us, and let us run with endurance the race that is set before us, fixing our eyes on Jesus, the author and perfecter of faith, who for the joy set before Him endured the cross, despising the shame, and has sat down at the right hand of the throne of God. For consider Him who has endured such hostility by sinners against Himself, so that you will not grow weary and lose heart. (Hebrews 12:1–3)

Overview

- We are Kingdom citizens, here for the Lord's good pleasure (Ephesians 2:10). We are ambassadors for Christ.
- Share your story.
  - The redeemed of the Lord are to say so (Psalm 107:1–2).
  - Present the Gospel simply. We need to introduce people to Jesus.
  - Share through words and actions.
- Spend time on what matters.
  - Spend time on eternal, rather than petty matters.
  - Get to the root of the issue.
  - Ask probing questions.
  - Focus on one area at a time.
  - Don't expect too much.
  - Concede trivial matters.
  - Don't get bogged down in a language debate. Keep it simple.
  - Set boundaries and know when to stop.
  - Don't get angry.
- Be kind (Luke 6:31; Colossians 4:6; 1 Peter 3:15).
  - Bathe everything in kindness.
  - People are not the enemy.
- Expect persecution.
  - We are at war with Satan.
  - You will be persecuted, just as Jesus was.
  - Continue to walk in love (1 Peter 2:11–12).
  - Our God is the same now and forever, but we win no matter what (Romans 14:8; 2 Corinthians 5:8).
  - We should prepare for persecution.
  - Trust God.

- Love is the formula. When in doubt, look to Jesus.
- Meet people where they are.
- When persecuted, expect the grace of God.
- Learn to see all aspects of life from God's perspective.
- Fix our eyes on Jesus (Hebrews 12:1–3).

Discussion Questions

1. Throughout this series, have your thoughts and emotions toward homosexuals changed?
2. Which suggestions from this chapter seem particularly relevant to you?
3. How can your church apply these suggestions?
4. What are you taking away from this series?

Additional Resources

Books

Butterfield, Rosaria Champagne. *Secret Thoughts of an Unlikely Convert.* Pittsburg: Crown & Covenant Publications, 2012.

Dallas, Joe. *The Gay Gospel?.* Eugene: Harvest House Publishers, 2007.

DeYoung, Kevin. *What Does the Bible Really Teach About Homosexuality?* Wheaton: Crossway, 2015.

Jernigan, Dennis. *Sing Over Me.* Collierville, TN: Innovo Publishing, 2014.

Moore, Russell. *Onward: Engaging the Culture without Losing the Gospel.* Nashville: B&H Books, 2015.

Films

Jernigan, Dennis. *Sing Over Me.* Directed by Jacob Kindberg. Free Verse Films, 2014, http://www.singovermemovie.com/.

Websites

Dennis Jernigan. http://dennisjernigan.com/needhelp.
Hope for Wholeness Network. http://www.hopeforwholeness. org/.

Joe Dallas. http://joedallas.com/.
Restored Hope Network. http://www.restoredhopenetwork. com/.

The Ethics & Religious Liberty Commission of the Southern Baptist Convention. http://erlc.com.
Robert Gagnon. http://www.robgagnon.net/ ChristianSexualityArticle.htm.

ADDITIONAL DENNIS JERNIGAN TITLES

www.innovopublishing.com

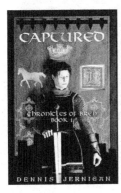